8/18/81
SKIP:
WITH SINCERE APPRECIATION!
HURRY BACK —
WE LOVE JOSTEN'S FOLKS!
Reed

[illegible] hope. [illegible] powered [illegible] hotel. We much enjoyed [illegible] as [illegible] you.
Thanks
Don.

Skip -
Rarely have I enjoyed working with a group as much as with you. Your people were fantastic. Come back soon!
J. Latta

dear skip,
what can i say? as i sit here with my Jostens pen in hand and think about your program all i can remember is laughing constantly! Thank you not only for the business but for making it such fun to take care of you! This book is to remind you of a beautiful city waiting for you to return!
Lots of Love,
Sabrina

To the most pleasant group that I've ever worked with
Greg

SKIP:
NOW YOU KNOW I'M NOT FULL OF — — —. I HOPE WE MEET YOUR EXPECTATIONS.
SINCERELY
Tom Baird

Skip
I was very nice working with you
Thanks
Mare Young

Portland Marriott Hotel

"Good citizens are the riches of a city."

Beautiful
Portland

Text by Robin Will

First Printing April, 1979
Published by Beautiful America Publishing Company
P.O. Box 608, Beaverton, Oregon 97005
Robert D. Shangle, Publisher

Library of Congress Cataloging in Publication Data
Beautiful Portland
1. Portland, Or.—Description—Views. I. Will, Robin, 1948-
F884.P.843B4 917.95'49 79-778

ISBN 0-915796-91-0 (hardbound)
ISBN 0-915796-90-2 (paperback)

Beautiful
Portland

BEAUTIFUL PORTLAND

A few years back, a report by the Midwest Research Institute, commissioned by the U.S. Environmental Protection Agency, named Portland, Oregon, the most liveable large city in the United States.

The report got a large and immediate reaction: trumpetings of promotional glee from areas that had scored high, dismay and sour grapes from cities unhappy with their position on the list. But Portland—at the top of the heap—received the news without enthusiasm. Portlanders already knew they lived in a great place, but they weren't sure they wanted the word to get out: they didn't want a flood of newcomers rushing in and spoiling things. Nobody went so far as to deny the truth of the study, but there was some uncomfortable squirming and words like "growth boundaries" began to appear in the press; and in the streets and businesses were heard these discouraging words: "They should have said something about the rain."

No one who knows Portland could be very surprised by that reaction. It's not modesty that makes Portlanders reticent—far from it; nor unfriendliness—visitors seldom find them so. But a certain weight of self-satisfaction is part of the Portland style: Oregonians in general have a "Garden of Eden" complex about their state. They like it the way it is, and they fear that any change will be for the worse. They always have. Like the rain and the general . . . well, *homeyness* of the place, the desire to be left alone and a slight anti-growth bias are definite Portland attributes.

Nor is it particularly surprising that Portlanders mentioned rain in an effort to dampen visitors' enthusiasm. Had it not been for roses, rain would probably have had a good change of becoming the city's symbol: it's an affliction that Portlanders embrace with a certain pride. Rain waters their gardens, and Portland owes much of its reputation as a city of gardens to the wet stuff from the sky. It also provides something to talk about: Portlanders complain about rain when it's falling, speculate about it when it isn't . . . and if the rain stays away too long you'll hear Portlanders wishing it would come back. And finally, natives use the subject of rain to scare off outsiders. "Portland is a nice enough place to live," natives will tell you, "but the rain will drive you crazy."

Portland's claim to distinction in the rain department rests on a sort of technicality: the city excels in duration rather than sheer quantity. Her average 41-inch rainfall puts the Rose City even with New York City, slightly ahead of Dallas-

Fort Worth's 35 inches, and way behind New Orleans, Nashville and Charleston, who respectively wade through 47, 48 and 49 inches a year. But in Portland it takes 150 days, on the average, for that average 41 inches to fall. New Yorkers get their precipitation in 113 days, and that's counting snowfall; and New Orleans' 47 inches come in less than 100 days. So without having the most rain, Portlanders enjoy more rainy days than almost anybody in an American city.

That's still something to brag about—or to complain, depending on the frame of reference, and people do both. The James G. Blaine Society—that mythical Oregon-for-the-Oregonians group—is like most myths: stronger than you might expect. Blainers complain . . . as long as there's a visitor within earshot. Others, enjoying the soporific effect of the rain and the lushness of growing things, don't say much at all. Either way, it's part of the Portland style.

There has been plenty said about the Portland style in the last hundred years or so, and the talking isn't done yet. There are people—and some of them even live there—who claim that the words ''Portland Style'' constitute a contradiction in terms. Others admit that there is such a thing as a Portland style; and deplore it. Still others, a complacent majority, can find no cause to complain. If the town doesn't exactly scintillate, it's of small concern to those who spend their free time in the mountains or at the ocean. If the city life, in the words of the old song, is ''built for comfort, not built for speed,'' who would want it to change? Who is against comfort? Actually, the style that Portland has accumulated in the last 130 years is rich and subtle, and has a lot to do with the vaunted ''liveability'' of the place.

One aspect of Portland's style that wins comment from almost every visitor is the pace. It is slow. Authors Terence O'Donnell and Thomas Vaughan . . . a pair of shrewd observers . . . make note of the fact in their book *Portland, A Historical Sketch and Guide.* ''Portland has never bustled. It doesn't today. It ambles . . . with some loitering on the way.'' There have always been individuals of energy and ambition in Portland but, Vaughan and O'Donnell note, ''The weight of the town's content usually defeats them.'' The folks who are ready to pronounce Portland dead after living there six months are frequently heard a few years later—still in town—telling horror stories about a trip to some other city. Creeping contentment gets to them.

''The weight of the town's content'' manifests itself in other ways, as well. ''Portland is a city of fine homes,'' commented one disgruntled connoisseur of nightlife, ''and that's where you find people after 8:00 at night.'' That is no longer as true as it once was: there's an excellent local music scene in pubs and lounges, and competition keeps standards high for the wine-dine-and-dance crowd. Both daily newspapers carry notices of other activities, and nightlife would seem to be about equal in quantity and quality to any other place Portland's size. Still, the city does not glitter, either socially or commercially, at night.

What Portlanders seem to do for entertainment and a sense of well-being is play outdoors. It is a tradition—and an easy one to understand considering the mild climate and the array of activities the natural setting offers. The city supports more garden clubs per capita than any other in the nation, and three of them, concerning roses, primroses and rhododendrons, have achieved national stature. Mt. Hood—seldom called anything but "the mountain" by Portlanders—was first climbed in 1857, and the Mazamas, local alpine club of long standing, celebrated their formation in 1894 with an ascent of nearly 200 people. Today there's skiing on the mountain, and the Mazamas, and others, are still climbing it. Boating excursions on the river and bicycling excursions on land were immensely popular at the turn of the century, and scenic drives were a principal recreation of those less inclined to exercise. About the only thing Portland has now that it didn't have in the old days is joggers, but on balance, early Portlanders enjoyed walking as a means of transportation and recreation. "After changes upon changes," as the song goes, "we are more or less the same."

Other aspects of the Portland style survive in spirit if not in form from the pioneering days of the Northwest. One, perhaps derived from the outdoorsy emphasis of the place, is a certain casualness and lack of ostentation that folks occasionally find disarming, and sometimes offensive. An Englishman with impeccable manners and a tendency to wear a necktie on any trips longer than a walk to the mailbox confessed that Portland—and the Northwest—took him quite aback. "I've never seen a place so informal," he said. "My banker came to call on me, and from his clothes I couldn't tell if he was there on business, or leaving on a fishing trip." Though other experiences might give a different picture of Portland bankers, executives in southwest Portland have been known to keep boats moored under the Sellwood Bridge for lunch-hour fishing trips. Our Englishman's confusion could be justified. It's hard to say whether the practice is still going on, but it's hard to think of a reason why it should have stopped.

Another testy reaction from out-of-town came to the engaging and wholesome tradition of a pub crawl to raise funds for the Portland Opera Association. "They're never going to get Portland out of the sticks," were the exact words of this sophisticate, although he may have changed his mind after actually going to the opera. One wonders if that's what an observer had in mind when he commented on the Portlanders' tendency to "prefer cultivation to sophistication." It sounds something like the tone of the 1870s, when gentlemen of status belonged not to posh clubs but to volunteer fire departments, and the firehouses had the best parties and dances in town. Portland has had its share of "respectability," but it usually feels imported: the casualness and informality is homegrown.

Even Portland's architecture tends to be almost casual, although in some very grand ways. Portland has always been known as a city of homes and gardens, not factories, skyscrapers or apartments. Persons of wealth have built magnificent homes, to be sure, but Portlanders have always tended to feel that ostentation was in poor taste. "Substantial comfort and tasteful display," was the way editor Harvey Scott characterized Portland's nicer homes at the turn of the century, as opposed to the "stoney" grandeur of New York or the "pre-eminent extravagance" of San Francisco. Portland homes have tended to look like homes rather than castles.

The glaring exception to this practice is the Pittock Mansion, a French chateau built by *Oregonian* publisher Henry Pittock. Terence O' Donnell and Thomas Vaughan deliver the final judgement in their little guidebook, some years after the fact: "this is not a very 'Portland' house," they comment rightly, noting that " . . . the town has always tended to look down its nose at splurge." Though the mansion is indeed "not very 'Portland'," Portlanders love it, and saved it from the wrecking ball in the 1960s, turning it into a city park. Its grounds now complete a nine-mile greenbelt through the heart of the city, and the house and its grounds are open to tours, meetings, and occasional civic receptions.

The grey-and-turreted mansion may be a little rich for Portland's blood, too grand for the arbiters of Portland's style, but Portlanders love it anyway. As such the big house is one of a number of things that people are "surprised" to find in Portland, as good a symbol as any of the disparity that somehow fits within the city's style. Portlanders have a tendency toward self-deprecation that makes them express surprise at homegrown excellence: a good building, a good school, prominent people, good music or good ideas. But it's hard to see how the surprise is warranted. For all the conservative, wholesome, outdoorsy, self-satisfied isolationism of the place, Portland has never been quite bucolic. One can imagine the city fathers climbing the mountain, planting rosebushes, managing lumber and tugboat companies; but at the same time—perhaps in those long, rainy winter evenings—the Multnomah County Library, Oregon Historical Society, and Oregon Symphony took root and grew. It's a problem, perhaps, of confusing style with content; at any rate, the mansion as well as other institutions and people in the city have in common the fact that they don't appear to fit.

The venerable Skidmore Fountain prompted critical surprise in an earlier century for similar reasons: it seemed a little too nice to be stuck in a town square in Portland. When pioneer druggist and city councilman Stephen Skidmore left a legacy to finance a public fountain, the city went straight to the top for a designer. Olin

(continued on page 26)

HILTON HOTEL

(Preceding page) The bronze drinking fountains in downtown Portland were a gift of lumberman Simon Benson. To the left is the Hilton Hotel, and in the background can be seen Jackson Tower, its clock a downtown landmark for many years.

(Opposite) Rose fanciers may choose their favorites from among the 10,000 varieties displayed in Washington Park's Rose Test Garden.

(Right) The Skidmore Fountain, a symbol of Old Portland, stands at the intersection of S.W. First and Ankeny.

(Below) The "working" portion of the Willamette River is north of downtown, near Swan Island. This view is from North Willamette Boulevard near the University of Portland.

(Left) Late afternoon sun highlights the Vista House at Crown Point in this view of the Columbia Gorge.

(Following page, above) Portland's Transit Mall restricts private auto traffic in the heart of downtown.

(Following page, below) Good weather brings a colorful flotilla to the Columbia River, near the Interstate Bridge.

(Second following page) The First National Bank looms at the end of this tree-lined walk in Lownsdale Square, one of the city's oldest parks.

(Preceding pages) The graceful arch of the Ross Island Bridge frames this view of downtown Portland at night, the city lights forming irridescent patterns on the water.

(Left) These aquatic frolickers, larger than life, grace the entry plaza of the Georgia Pacific building.

(Below) A replica of the Liberty Bell occupies a place of honor in O'Bryant Square, across from Portland's City Hall.

(Opposite) Washington Park's Rose Test Gardens command a fine view of Mt. Hood.

(Left) It's weather and water against stone at Cape Kiwanda in Tillamook County, where pounding waves foam against the foot of the cape.

(Following page, above) Flattening effect of the telephoto lens superimposes images of the Morrison, Hawthorne, Marquam and Ross Island Bridges as a tug pushes a gravel-laden barge upriver.

(Following page, below) The stately and symmetrical Pittock Mansion and its hilltop gardens became a city park in the 1960s.

(Second following page) A scattering of leaves suggests the beginning of autumn along this quiet path in Laurelhurst Park.

(Third following page) Newer buildings in downtown Portland are set back from the street, providing room for plantings and quiet courtyards like this one at Standard Plaza. In the background, the Georgia Pacific Building rises behind Multnomah County Courthouse.

Warner's fountain drew reviews from as far away as New York. "The fact that Warner's figures look calmly down upon buggies and buckboards, and shirt-sleeves and slouch hats in Oregon, instead of decorating Central Park (in New York) is grotesquely significant of much," commented *Scribner's* magazine in a rather petty tone. It was as if New York was surprised that Portland had come up with the money, let alone the good taste, to put up something really handsome in a public square.

Just before the unveiling, brewer Henry Weinhard made what seems in retrospect a very Portland offer. He would run a firehose 11 blocks down from the brewery so that the Skidmore could flow with beer on its first day. The response was equally Portland; Weinhard's offer was politely declined.

On another level, some people have expressed surprise that Reed College is so much at home in Portland. In the early 'Teens of this century, when Reed was founded, Portland was a bastion of aggressive wholesomeness, conservatism, and respectability. Some say it still is. Reed College, based on the idea that ". . . most hallowed traditions are petrified errors . . ." must have seemed radical, unconventional, or both; and it was virtually unknown for a college to be without church affiliation. Still, Oregon has an inexplicable reputation for harboring mavericks—colleges or public officials, and for mixing up liberalism and conservatism in strange ways. It is possible to approve of liberal Reed College—or Wayne Morse or Tom McCall—for conservative reasons, apparently, and Oregonians have figured out how to do it.

Portland is finishing the 20th century with style, and even in this electronic era of bland standardization, the Portland style is wearing well. The smugness and isolationism are not as obvious as they once were: no city is as isloated and as self-sufficient as it once was. And as for that self-satisfaction, well . . . things began to slip in Portland in the 50s and 60s, and people have begun to realize that liveability is a series of decisions and not a place on the map. But the new decisions and directions don't look too unusual in light of Portland's past. Old Town is rejuvenating, downtown is growing with as much deliberation as a city can summon in an age when everything happens fast . . . even in Portland. Across the river, the image of Portland as a city of homes and gardens is being dusted off, patched and repainted. Suburban life loses its appeal compared to a city that was meant to be lived in, and that's what Portland is about. The resurgence of interest in Irvington, Laurelhurst, Albina, Eastmoreland, Hollywood, the Alameda, Sellwood, Sabin, Sunnyside,

(Preceding page, above) Swan Island, foreground, was once the site of Portland's airport, and is now a busy shipping and industrial center. In the background is the Fremont Bridge and the skyline of downtown.

(Preceding page, below) Visitors may wander through about four acres of plantings in the International Rose Test Gardens at Washington Park. Mt. Hood is in background.

Brooklyn, Montavilla and Woodstock, with their neighborhood associations, seems a guarantee that a comfortable city is still held in high esteem.

Portlanders know what they've got. They can suffer complaints about the night life, the slowness of pace, the intellectual climate, and the "style" with equanimity, knowing that, in the words of Judge Matthew Deady, they live in a town where people "sleep sounder and live longer." And Portlanders probably don't need to fear those influxes of outsiders in search of liveability in the rain. They'll be defeated by the weight of the town's content—they'll become Portlanders, too.

THE PHYSICAL SETTING

Portland's founding fathers had shrewd foresight—or extreme good luck—when they decided against most popular opinion to locate a town on that last bend in the Willamette. The townsite has proven itself profitable for one set of reasons, and loveable for another set, a combination of beauty and utility not every city can claim. A great deal of the style of the town has been conditioned by the easy access to countryside, mountains and the ocean, an inevitability which few find cause to regret.

In the middle-1840s, the reasons for putting a town there were not clear—especially to residents of Fort Vancouver and Oregon City, the "real" settlements in the Oregon Country. "Stumptown," they called it derisively, since no one had found time for such formalities as dragging the stumps out of the streets. (It should be added however, that the city government did have them whitewashed, so they'd be easier to see at night).

Stumps or not, a town has to do business to survive, and Portland found itself with two great natural assets and a widening marketplace while still very young. The river was the first: Captain John Couch, apparently after some trouble upstream on the gravel shoals at Oregon City, decided that Portland was the actual head of deep-water navigation on the Willamette, and staked his claim near Asa Lovejoy's at the bend in the river. The other early-day asset was the Great Plank Road that Daniel Lownsdale built through a wooded canyon west of Portland into the fertile Tualatin Valley. The valley had been settled for some time, and grain had been grown there, but the valley's isolation prevented any real marketing of its produce. Today it takes a

(Left) Autumn has left a touch of color in the maple leaves, in this view of Mt. Hood from high in the Mt. Hood National Forest.

stretch of the imagination to recall the physical barriers between Portland and Hillsboro, but the water route down the Tualatin River to the Willamette involved a portage around the falls at Oregon City, and overland travel on such roads as existed was a joke during the rather extensive rainy season. The Plank Road—today's Canyon Road—linked the area's richest food producing region with the area's only deep-water port. Indian wars inland, and gold rushes in Oregon, Washington, California and Alaska brought the market: ships, men and money poured into the new port, and the town prospered.

The Willamette is still Portland's greatest business asset, though it's not as easy to see as it once was. For a look at the "working" end of the river, you should get over to Mock's Crest in North Portland for a drive along Willamette Boulevard. Two things will be accomplished by such a pilgrimage, and maybe more, depending on the time spent meandering through the pleasant neighborhood that stretches back from the crest into St. Johns. The first thing is that the crest is a great place to get an overall view of the part of the Willamette that pays the bills. Directly below is Swan Island, once the site of the Portland airport and now the locus of port and industrial activity, including drydocks. This is one of the longest river views in town, lined on both banks with grain elevators and ships, the Fremont Bridge arching gracefully overall and the towers of downtown rising behind. (If you want to get a closer look, call the Port of Portland, and they'll tell you about tours.) The other thing the trip will accomplish is to put you just about in the place where William Clark stood for one of the first views of the Portland area by a white man. He was not able to see far upriver because of what he called "mist." That part of history, at least, is re-enacted continuously in Portland, and on foggy days it's possible to get exactly the same view that Lewis and Clark had.

But early Portland wasn't all work and no play, and it isn't today. If a river is big enough to float a log raft, it's big enough to put a rowboat in and go fishing, or just exploring the wooded riverbanks, upstream at first so you can drift home with the current after a hard day of rowing. And the river wasn't the only attraction. "The mountain" was a harrowing 60 miles away on such roads as there were, and people visited it regularly. Some of them summered there. The Columbia River Highway and attendant parks opened in 1915 to the delight of Portlanders, to whom scenic drives were already a way of life. And Portlanders went to the ocean by the trainload.

Improved travel and increased leisure have had the effect of expanding the Portlander's range beyond hills, rivers and mountain. The site of the city is still a beautiful place, and pleasure boats dot both the Willamette and Columbia. But Portland is made all the more attractive by the features within two or three hours' drive of the city. A 100-mile drive from Portland—two hours or so—can take the traveler to: anywhere on the coast between Astoria and Newport; down the Willamette Valley almost to Eugene; beyond the snow-capped and forested Cascades to the high, dry (and sunny!) country of Central Oregon; up the mighty Columbia Gorge as far as the John Day Dam; or into Washington as far as Mt. Rainier, Olympia, and the tip of Puget Sound. The 100-mile radius takes in three mountains higher than 9,000 feet and a score of smaller ones, two Indian reservations, a sizeable piece of seacoast rich in scenery and natural bounty, and a few hundred miles of one of the world's great rivers.

The Portlander has only to choose a destination and go. A drive through the lushly-wooded Coast Range ends at the ocean, where one can spend a day, a week—or a lifetime—exploring. On land are found towns, parks, hiking trails of great or small duration, fishing and camping. The sea offers a variety of experience for folks who charter boats or bring their own. Land and sea meet in a rich environment where, depending on location, waves may beat themselves to froth against rocky cliffs, where tidepools teem with the life of the sea: starfish, sea anenome, comical hermit crabs. You might catch a glimpse of a sea otter floating on his back in the turbulent water without concern, clutching a clam to his chest with one forepaw and hammering it with a rock held in the other. The wide-open, sandy beaches offer different sport: clambering in the driftwood (stay away from driftwood in the water!), fishing in the surf, throwing a frisbee, flying a kite, or just doing some creative loafing.

In the other direction are the Cascades, with downhill and cross-country skiing in the winter, camping and hiking in the National Forests in summer; and beyond the Cascades, the rivers, lakes, forests and scenery of high-and-dry Central Oregon—like a different state entirely. You'll know you're getting there when, crossing the mountains, you see pines instead of firs and less brush on the floor of the forest. The Cascades form a giant rain-trap, not letting clouds over until they have dropped some of their rainy burden, so on the east side of the mountains the rain-forest aspect disappears, and pine-covered slopes drop to dry and almost flat land covered with sagebrush and juniper.

The high valley floor is carved in places with deep river gorges, creating rugged rimrock vistas which open suddenly to surprise the traveler who thought he was on the plains. Lakes, natural and artificial, the snow-capped Cascades, and parks and national forests beyond enumeration make this a fine contrast to the lushness of the Willamette Valley. And further east is drier land yet—wheat and cattle country, for the most part, but it's outside of easy driving distance from Portland and a line needs to be drawn somewhere . . . .

(Following pages) Moody clouds gather over downtown Portland in this view from the southwest hills.

Of course, the alternative to choosing a destination and hitting the road is *not* choosing a destination and hitting a road. Stay off of freeways and well-traveled secondaries and just meander. Stop at small-town historical museums and county parks, antique shops, livestock auctions and historical markers. Remember that nobody gives prizes for the distance you cover, and that some mighty pretty farmland and interesting local attractions lie within a relatively few miles of the city.

There is no way to sum up the variety of experience that is available to the traveler who uses Portland as a home base, and little use to try. Many books are available on different areas and activities in the state, and if a traveler doesn't want to trust to luck, he should pinpoint a specific interest and buy one. (Then, on the other hand, he should be prepared not to follow the book too closely: serendipity will take you where a guidebook can't). But there are some general, and perhaps obvious, things that can be said about the country around Portland that might explain it. Or might help explain Portland.

First of all, since Portland is the region's principal city, you leave the city environment when you leave Portland. You will find other lively, though smaller, towns; then some much-smaller towns; then villages, picturesque hamlets, spreads of fat-looking farmland . . . and wilderness. For years Oregon's output could be expressed in two terms: agriculture and timber, and that is easy to read in the character of land outside of town. Portland is a city with easily accessible rural roots, and this is where you find them.

Although leaving town doesn't mean leaving civilization (in fact, some folks will tell you quite the opposite) it means that the destination you have in mind is likely to be a natural one in some sense of the word. To whatever extent you like, you will be dealing with phenomena of nature rather than people and institutions. You may find a state park located to preserve a waterfall or a canyon, making it more accessible to the public; or a national forest with miles of trails to places the public will probably never see. You may water-ski, row or paddle on a stretch of quiet water, or simply find a place out of the wind to sit and watch the ocean. Whatever you do, odds are that you'll do it outdoors.

A further point about this rural, natural, outdoor activity is that you don't have to spend a lot of money doing it. A day hike, a fishing trip, inner-tubing on a white-water river or a solitary walk by the ocean can all be accomplished with a minimum of cash and equipment—and you can still be home in time for dinner. If you don't *want* to be home for dinner, there are motels and also places to camp in state parks. If you want to *catch* your dinner, fishing licenses are not expensive; or for the price of a tide-table, a shovel and a gunnysack you can dig a mess of clams. The possibilities are endless, and they're all within reach.

Old Town Downtown Uptown

At one time, all of Portland—business, residential and industrial—fit neatly in the flat space between the river and the West Hills with room to spare. That was a long time ago, but remnants of all are still visible, and in one area—Goose Hollow—the name commemorates an even more distant time when the west side had farms, and flocks of geese, and battles among farmwives over their ownership. The geese exist in memory only, and one suspects in general that the old city may have been more interesting than the one we have today. In the old days there was much less ''zoning,'' and it was common to find homes, boarding-houses, restaurants and saloons, business and industry cheek-by-jowl downtown. In the days when people walked a lot or took streetcars, there were also more people on the streets—at all hours—than we're likely to see today.

Today the metropolis called ''Stumptown'' can be divided into a few districts that speak to historic interest as well as activities of the present. ''Uptown'' was the city's nicest neighborhood, separated from Old Town by Slabtown. Downtown is the direction everything has been heading since sometime before the turn of the century.

A bit of West Side geography will probably help with orientation, and the main point to keep in mind—as always—is that Portland is located on a bend in the river. The earliest grid of streets was laid out parallel to the Willamette. The city's first structure was a log cabin on the riverbank at the foot of Washington Street, and the new town straggled up and downriver from there, with northward development mostly business, and development toward the south mostly residential. But a few blocks north of Washington, the river bends to the west, so in later development northward, streets were oriented to the compass. The two grids meet along West Burnside, creating some unusual intersections, some funny-shaped buildings, and, towards the river, one interesting plaza wherein stands the Skidmore Fountain.

The venerable fountain, dating from 1888, marks what once was the center of Portland's business district. It stands in an irregularly-shaped intersection where S.W.

(Following page) Specimens like this make the Rose Gardens a delightful place for a meandering walk.

PACIFIC TRADER
MONROVIA

Ankeny intersects with Front Avenue, in the shadow of the Burnside Bridge. At one time it was surrounded on the landward side by the arched, corniced and iron-ornamented Italianate facades of a busy "downtown;" on the river side, by warehouses and sheds with wharves on the water. When Councilman Skidmore made the bequest for a fountain, he specified utility as one of its attributes—"for men, dogs and horses"—and few locations could have served better than this one.

But the city center didn't stay there. Between fires and floods in the 1870s, 80s and 90s, many businessmen found not only motive but opportunity to build on higher ground. The Burnside Bridge, built in 1926, leaves the ground at Third Avenue for its leap across the river, making traffic flow in the old part of town difficult indeed. Then in 1929, the riverside wharves and warehouses were demolished and the seawall built. The Skidmore Fountain area, deprived of traffic, commerce and activity of the river, began to decay.

Today the area is known as Old Town. In the 1960s, some courageous businessmen started moving back. They recognized the value of the solid old buildings and the sense of neighborhood that the old district provided, and they began to draw people back onto the streets in Old Town. Other businesses followed, including some of the small and wonderful places that can't survive in the high-rent district of downtown, but which add a touch that the main-stream merchants are hard put to supply. Saturday Market came along and proved that something could be done with the space under the bridge—and after a gap of some fifty or sixty years, there was once again an open-air market in Old Town, and crowds of people in the plaza around the Skidmore Fountain.

The Skidmore Fountain's block is a little gappy, like the rest of Old Town. Much was destroyed before Portlanders realized its value, and old photographs provide the best way to realize the real people-scaled grandeur of the old plaza. Still, though the place had an interesting past, it also has a lively present. The firms that operate here do so because there's real value to the place, not just historical cuteness, and they save Old Town from the preciousness that afflicts some historic neighborhoods that are allowed to exist only as tourist traps.

Other areas north of Burnside are worth noting. One is Slabtown, a working-class residential district that is barely surviving the age of the automobile and the truck. It lies to the north and west of the Old Town core. Its name derives from the old-time practice of buying slabwood from sawmills for fuel, and stacking it at the curb in front of the house: in "nicer" neighborhoods it wasn't done. Slabtown

(Preceding page, above) From the hills of northwest Portland, the Fremont Bridge appears to challenge Washington's Mt. St. Helens for dominance of the skyline.

(Preceding page, below) The Pacific Trader *docks to load grain near the Broadway Bridge.*

separated Old Town from Uptown, which was once called "West End" or "Nob Hill." It's the area where the street numbers are in the high teens and twenties, between Burnside and about Lovejoy, where Portland's wealthy people lived before the West Hills became desirable real estate. That was a long time ago, but some of the gracious old homes remain, and Uptown culminates in a shopping center where Vista, Burnside, 23rd and Westover intersect. Before Prohibition, there was a brewery there.

The problems of flooding and fire were certainly forces that helped move Portland's main business district back from its riverfront beginnings. Portlanders were good sports about the periodic flooding, holding regattas and parades when water was four feet deep in the streets, but humor eventually wore thin and the only reasonable thing to do was build on higher ground. In the 1870s, when the Pioneer Courthouse was built on 5th Avenue between Morrison and Yamhill, Portlanders decried it for being too far out of town. Photographs of the new building do, indeed, show a milk cow wandering in the street. But by the time 20 years had passed, it was clear that the planners had planned aright.

Still, it took years for expansion to eradicate the residential nature of southwest Portland, and some traces are still there. The Corbett home stubbornly held out—an island of tree-shaded graciousness with a cow tethered out back—until 1936 on the site of the Greyhound Depot. The Ladd home gave way for the *Oregonian* building on Broadway between Jefferson and Columbia, but in a stroke of luck the Ladd Carriage House remains across Broadway, an enormous pile of Victorian frippery which now houses offices. The Jacob Kamm house was to be sacrificed for the new Lincoln High School, but Eric Ladd moved it to a site near S.W. 20th and Jefferson. Gracious homes once lined the South Park Blocks as well, but the last one—an enormous, white-pillared affair—came out when Portland State enlarged Cramer Hall in the late 1960s.

The Park Blocks themselves are 'very Portland,' having managed to preserve almost intact for more than 125 years the will and vision of the town fathers who set the land aside for a park in 1852. Not much of the Portland of that period has survived except for these blocks, and they have worn exceedingly well. Originally there were 25 of them, stretching from the hills down to Ankeny, making a slight dogleg where Southwest becomes Northwest, and then heading for the river. In the 1870s eight blocks in the middle fell into private hands and were built upon, but

(Following page, above) Plantings and promenades distinguish the new waterfront park which stretches from the Burnside Bridge, above, south to the Hawthorne Bridge.

(Following page, below) A snowy night adds to the intrigue of the lights in the Tualatin Valley, looking west from Council Crest.

(Preceding page) Sacajawea, heroine of the Lewis and Clark Expedition, is honored by a statue in Washington Park.

(Opposite) Underwater lights accentuate the cataracts of the Forecourt Fountain, an inner-city park, while evening darkens the skies over Portland.

(Right) Quiet solitude prevails at Skyline Memorial Gardens.

(Below) The Japanese Gardens are tucked into a quiet wooded retreat on a hilltop in Washington Park.

(Following pages) A full moon rises over Portland at twilight as the city's lights start to come on.

(Third following page, above) Chamber musicians perform in the Shakespearean Garden, Washington Park.

(Third following page, below) Greenery and the sound of running water provide diversion from the city's backdrop at Standard Plaza.

HILTON

(Preceding page) This exemplary specimen of Portland's favorite flower was photographed in Washington Park.

(Left) Portlanders who get up early may be treated to a sunrise like this one, photographed from high in Forest Park.

(Left) Shemanski Fountain stands at the foot of the Park Blocks.

(Below) Venerable Jackson Tower, with its clock on top, seems dwarfed by newcomers on the Portland skyline.

(Opposite) Lights of Portland sparkle on a snowy evening, in this view looking east from Council Crest.

(Following page, above) The older section of downtown Portland serves as a backdrop for a crew team practicing on the smooth river.

(Following page, below) The Pioneer Courthouse is at the heart of downtown Portland. The Meier and Frank Building rises behind.

THE
OREGON BANK

ROSENB
Shops

(Preceding page) Brick sidewalks, bus-stop shelters and plantings are part of the "new" downtown of the Transit Mall.

(Right) Flowerbaskets add a splash of color to the dignified facades of Old Town.

(Below) Oregon Museum of Science and Industry (OMSI) and the Kendall Planetarium occupy a site in Portland's West Hills adjoining the Zoo.

(Following page) The Hawthorne Bridge is the oldest of the ten auto bridges that cross the Willamette in Portland.

(Second following page) Mt. Hood seems to hover above the waters of the Columbia in this view from a sailboat outing on the river.

excepting that tragedy this elm-lined break in pavement and traffic has been preserved, from S.W. Jackson down to S.W. Salmon, and again from Ankeny to the Post Office on N.W. Hoyt.

The Park Blocks resemble a corridor of greenery through the downtown district, and that is how they're frequently used. No matter where a person is in southwest Portland, it is an easy matter to walk up to the park and saunter under the trees to your destination. It's one of Portland's favorite detours for the traveler on foot. In the early days, this park—rather far from the city's core—was a dirt track where young men could race their buggies, and when the park was "civilized," planted to elms and grass, townhouses began to appear on its edges. Today Portland State University straddles the south end of the Park Blocks. A stroll downhill toward the city center will take you past several churches, the magnificent headquarters of the Oregon Historical Society and Portland Art Museum (take time to visit the sculpture mall between the museum and the Masonic Temple).

Some impressive statuary of the civic kind has found its way into the Park Blocks as well. Rough-Rider Theodore Roosevelt sits astride a horse in the block across which the Historical Society and the Art Museum face. A block to the north, an introspective Abraham Lincoln seems to recall the Civil War years, and in the next block stand the graceful Shemanski Fountain and a small tiled plaza devoted to one of the Benson fountains.

No matter what a book includes or ignores about downtown Portland, it is obligatory to mention the Benson fountains. The bronze, four-bowl pedestal-style drinking fountains in evidence throughout the downtown area were a gift to the city in 1917 by Simon Benson, a lumberman, philanthropist and entrepreneur. A number of stories exist to explain the gift, and although none can be verified, they're all good. One is that Benson was touched by the cries of a thirsty child during a Rose Festival parade; another claims that Benson himself, thirsty while walking in downtown Portland, could find among the saloons nowhere to get a glass of water; and yet another suggests that Benson, a practical man, simply wanted his loggers to have some alternative to grogeries if mere thirst was an issue. All that's known for sure is that he did, indeed, give them. The fountains are a cherished local institution, ranking right up with roses, the rain and Mt. Hood in the affections of Portlanders.

In recent years, nothing has changed the face of downtown Portland as much as the Transit Mall. It is a forward-looking attempt to free the civic center from the

(Preceding page, above) The mast of the battleship Oregon, *a distinguished fighter in the Spanish-American War, now reposes on the river bank esplanade as a memorial.*

(Preceding page, below) The peaceful beauty of Crystal Springs Lake does little for the peace of mind of golfers at Eastmoreland, one of the city's public golf courses.

grasp of the motorcar, and, as one might expect from a project intended to separate Americans from their automobiles, the completed project is still a matter of contention. Ironically, the mall, in resolving a contemporary problem, utilizes a form which townspeople of pre-automobile days would have found quite agreeable. From Portland State north to Everett Street, and from the river to 13th, travel by Tri-Met bus is free, in exchange for which auto traffic is limited in a two-by-twelve block area in the city's core. Once Portlanders master this last aspect, frustration should ease. In the meantime, downtowners are already enjoying the wide brick sidewalks, the sculpture, trees, benches and even the bus-stop shelters that grace the downtown mall. Nothing could be more "Portland" in tradition than public transportation—reminiscent of the excellent streetcar system of the old days—and foot travel downtown.

(Following page, above) Western Forestry Center, part of the Zoo/OMSI complex, contains exhibits relating to forestry and lumbering in the Northwest. The "high wheels" helped teams of horses or oxen drag huge logs from the woods.

(Following page, below) A log boom lies in the river near "5.1," the railroad bridge that is 5.1 miles out of Portland's Union Station.

THE PARKS

One of Portland's firmly-ingrained traditions is the building of parks. Why this should have been the case in the early days is open to speculation. Everything was new and fresh then, and with the town strung out along the riverbank, there could have been no shortage of open space. But luckily, our forefathers built parks, as we do today, and the result is a city of striking distinctions in the pleasant category of parklands. Ranking 40th in population of the 50 largest American cities, Portland nevertheless rates solidly in the top ten both in parkland compared to total area, and parkland per capita. Portland has the largest wilderness park totally within the limits of an American city. A notation in the *Guinness Book of Records* also gives Portland the honor of the world's smallest city park. The only extinct volcano within a city limits is—you guessed it—in a Portland city park. Large or small, grand or merely comfortable, there are altogether about 160 Portland city parks.

The reasons for this comparative splurge are not entirely clear. Perhaps Portlanders set aside parkland because, in the early days, they could not bear to be closed up in town, and so compensated by creating open spaces. Early photos of Portland suggest another reason: in the throes of early growth and construction, Portland had a cluttered and tacky appearance. Perhaps the good citizens were simply setting aside areas to be kept free of the debris of growth. Or perhaps Terence O'Donnell and Thomas Vaughan were correct, discussing Portland's curious emphasis on nature, in their comment that Portlanders ". . . do not particularly want an urban life, only its amenities." Whatever the reason, about one-eighth of the land in the city is devoted to public parks.

Perhaps the most amazing of the city parks are the oldest ones, if for no other reason than the fact that they exist at all. The downtown Park Blocks, discussed elsewhere, fit in this category, having been set aside in 1851, and so do the Plaza Blocks, dedicated in the same year. These blocks are between Third and Fourth Avenues, Salmon and Madison Streets; and are divided by S.W. Main Street, wherein stands a statue of an elk given to the city in 1900 by an ex-mayor. Real elk, in fact, used to graze in this riverside meadow before the city got too close. Today the original courthouse squares are joined by O'Bryant Square, a block to the south. They are enjoyed by office workers on lunch hours, and the area's elderly.

No less surprising is Washington Park, purchased by the city in 1871. At that time the park was far away from the city, but the Portland penchant for roses, scenic

(Preceding page) The rose was adopted as Portland's official symbol in the 1880s.

drives and romantic views found some of its earliest expression there. The park sat unimproved for the first ten years; then in the '80s a park keeper was appointed, plantings begin, and a small zoo was laid out. The fountain in the center of the park, near the Sacajawea statue, served as a watering-place for carriage horses overheated from the long pull up the hill, and the nearby reservoirs, bordered by wide walkways and railings, were designed as promenades. The view from the top of the hill has always been worth the trip: this panorama of city, river and mountain is *the* Portland view, no question about it.

Uphill and to the south of the fountain are tennis courts, an amphitheatre and the International Rose Test Gardens. The gardens provide a reminder that the Portland Rose Society, founded in 1888, is now the nation's oldest and largest rose society. Following a long-time tradition, the Gardens distribute free cuttings in the spring from the terraced plantings which, comprising about ten thousand varieties of roses, cover four acres. Beyond the Rose Test Gardens, there's a choice of routes. The uphill one takes the visitor eventually to the Japanese Gardens, a bit of serene beauty tucked between dark firs on a hilltop; and downhill a loop leads past an archery range in a big open meadow, above the reservoirs and back to the fountain. At the very top of Washington Park is the Zoo Train Station.

The Zoo Train is among the features for which the Portland Zoological Gardens are famous. It's a narrow-gauge railroad which carries passengers through the woods between Washington Park and the zoo site. Another feature of the zoo that has attracted national attention is the fecund nature of the elephant population. It has not been satisfactorily explained why elephants breed better in Portland than any other zoo in the world, but they do. Portland's zoo also gained short-term notoriety when the chimpanzees began painting pictures . . . and the pictures started making money! It was part of the zoo's Behavioral Enrichment Program. Other experiments allow primates to match their game-playing skills against zoo visitors via electronic machinery. Opinion on the value of all this is divided, but it gives the animals—and the zoo visitors—something to do. Adjacent to the Zoo is Oregon Museum of Science and Industry (OMSI) and the Western Forestry Center.

Today Washington Park, together with the Zoo-OMSI complex, form the southernmost portion of a network of parks that run continuously for almost nine miles to the northern city limit. These parks are adjoined on the north by the Hoyt Arboretum, with creeks, trails, picnic areas, and one of the nation's largest collections of conifers. Across Burnside Road, to the north, is Pittock Acres Park, the final link in the nine-mile greenbelt. This tract is home to the Pittock Mansion and its

(Left) Crystal Springs Rhododendron Gardens offer a feast of springtime floral color, and a peaceful vista across Crystal Springs Lake to Eastmoreland Golf Course.

gardens, and a splendid view that takes in Mts. Hood, St. Helens, Rainier, and sometimes others, as well as downtown and a vast length of the "working" portion of the river. North of Pittock Acres is Macleay Park, straddling Cornell Road, providing hills and trails on the south side, canyons and trails on the north. The Oregon Audubon Society Bird Sanctuary adjoins Macleay Park on the west; Forest Park adjoins it on the north. Forest Park runs north about six more miles, containing about 25 miles of hiking trails and more wilderness than you'll find in the limits of any American city. The Portland Park Bureau is happy to supply specific information.

In contrast to the wilderness of the places just named, Council Crest is a mannered, mowed and clipped eminence in the city's southwest hills. The crest was named in 1898 by a party of Congregational ministers and their wives who picnicked there one summer evening. At first a cable car, then a streetcar made the heights accessible to the city; homes were built there and an amusement park operated on Council Crest until the Depression of the 1930s. In 1937 the city traded an unused firehouse for the hilltop, and it became a city park. On clear days, the view is unequalled: the park commands almost all of Portland, the two rivers, five snowcapped mountains and—in the other direction—the Tualatin Valley as far as the Coast Range.

For anyone in the neighborhood, it's a short jaunt to two of the city's most popular scenic drives. One is S.W. Fairmount Boulevard, just downhill from Council Crest and encircling the whole hilltop. It was popular among the carriage and bicycle set at the turn of the century. Further down the east flank of the hill is Terwilliger Boulevard, the city's first and only parkway, then and now a series of sweeping curves bordered by tended lawns, romantic views and white lamp-posts.

South Portland—an old-time designation for the area beyond Jefferson Street—was the site of one of the nation's first urban renewal projects in the 1960s, and benefited greatly by the construction of three new parks, two of which contain fountains. Some of the newness has worn off, the plantings have begun to grow, and the parks have subsided into the Portland scene, although when they were new they attracted a great deal of local attention. The three sites together make up an easy stroll, and as elsewhere on the west side, it's a good idea to park the car and walk to—and through—them.

Starting at the south, on the river side of S.W. Fourth Avenue, is Lovejoy Park, a little plaza all of concrete with an incredible fountain that cascades down from a peak, through some "rapids" with stepping-stones, and into a broad, quiet pool. When the fountain was new there was controversy over whether it was meant to be waded in, or just looked at; but over the last dozen years everybody has relaxed and acknowledged that the park seems to welcome all kinds of participation.

Pettygrove Park is a short saunter away amid the high-rises. It was fitting to put Lovejoy and Pettygrove close together, since they were the pioneers who decided on Portland's name with a flip of the coin back in 1845. (Pettygrove won; Lovejoy wanted Boston). Pettygrove Park is a bumpy, densely planted landscape with meandering paths, and though it doesn't appear to be intended as a children's park, it does appeal to children of many ages.

Another stroll northward puts the visitor at the Civic Auditorium, with its magnificent Forecourt Fountain in front. Taking up about half the block in front of the Auditorium, this fountain—of plain grey concrete—resembles a mountain stream in its upper reaches and a dozen waterfalls in its lower. The whole display provides nooks, crannies, eddies and open spaces all echoing with the sound of moving water. Like its smaller companion piece, the Lovejoy, created by the same design firm, the Forecourt Fountain invites participation from waders and watchers.

Not last, but certainly least of the west-side parks, where size is concerned, is Mill Ends Park. This is different from other parks by virtue of its size, which is only about a foot in diameter, and by its intended clientele, which are leprechauns and others of such turn of mind as can enjoy a city park of this size. Mill Ends Park had its beginning when Dick Fagan, author of an *Oregon Journal* column by the same name, was gazing out his window in the old Journal building on a slow afternoon. He noticed a hole in the concrete median in Front Avenue, intended perhaps for a power pole but never used. Fagan put some flowers there, and wrote a column about it . . . and another, and another, describing happenings in the leprechaun community which gathered there. Fagan tended the park and wrote about it until his death in 1969, by which time the park had become a Portland tradition. Mill Ends Park became an official city park on St. Patrick's Day in 1977, and has been noted in the *Guinness Book of Records* as the world's smallest city park. It is located in the median strip on Front Avenue between Taylor and Yamhill. Parking is not available, and anyone bigger than a leprechaun should plan his visit during a time when traffic is light.

Across the river are parks of striking size and beauty as well. Laurelhurst Park—S.E. 39th and Stark—is the oldest of these, purchased in 1909, part of the Hazelfern farm of pioneer William Ladd. The park is full of magnificent trees, old plantings of rhododendron, and acres of rolling lawn, and at one end of the central

(Following page) More than 2,000 varieties of rhododendrons occupy a peninsula and an island in Crystal Springs Lake at the Rhododendron Gardens.

A269

ravine a pleasant lake is home for dozens of waterfowl. The neighborhood which surrounds the park is a treat in itself for strollers, joggers and bicyclists.

What William S. Ladd did for Laurelhurst, his son, William C., did for Eastmoreland by donating 40 acres of his Crystal Springs farm to Reed College for a campus. The community of Eastmoreland was developed around Reed College, trading heavily on the refinement and cultivation the college would have to offer. Whatever the circumstances, today Reed is a handsome and vital institution, while, across S.E. Woodstock Street, Eastmoreland is a handsome and vital community. But the real gem of the area is Crystal Springs Rhododendron Gardens.

The gardens are the result of a bargain struck between the city and the American Rhododendron Society in 1950. The city provided the land and one gardener, and the Society supplied the plantings and all the rest of the labor. Seldom has cooperation had more beautiful results. The park occupies a portion of the bank of Crystal Springs Lake, and an island in the middle, displaying about 2,000 rhododendrons as well as native firs and plantings of ornamental trees. A network of trails covers the island, allowing extensive meandering in a fairly limited space, and the dark firs, the reflecting surface of the lake and the brilliance of the plantings make this place unequalled in Portland. Things are at their colorful best on rare sun-drenched days in the early spring, but the moods of the garden are many and this park is never without attraction during the changing seasons. The lake is home to a variety of waterfowl who have figured out the benefits of year-round residence, and for a particularly warm welcome, visitors should take along a bag of bread crusts or bird seed.

Mt. Tabor, between S.E. Belmont and S.E. Division, has reservoirs at its feet, a park on its crown, and an amphitheatre in its crater—Mt. Tabor is the only extinct volcano within a city limit. Once a popular place to cruise in autos, at present, access to the top is by foot only. It's a pleasant walk, and downhill all the way back, two items one might consider for an evening's stroll. An exceedingly dour-looking Harvey W. Scott, illustrious *Oregonian* editor, stands at the top much larger than life, surveying the city he helped nurse, wheedle, cajole and lambaste into the 20th century. All around, the grassy slopes are shaded by immense firs which capture any breath of wind and murmur gently, their quiet wuthering providing a special kind of background to the sounds of the city.

(Preceding page, above) The Rough Rider, a statue of young Teddy Roosevelt, occupies a place of honor in the South Park Blocks in front of the Portland Art Museum.

(Preceding page, below) Rose Festival time brings ships of many nationalities to Portland to dock at the seawall.

PHOTO CREDITS

RAY ATKESON—*page 23, below; page 51; pages 64-65.*

JOHN GRONERT—*pages 12-13; pages 20-21; pages 28-29; pages 32-33.*

JOHN HILL—*page 15; pages 16-17; page 18, below; page 22, below; page 37, below; page 54, below; page 60, above; page 60, below; page 69, below.*

OREGON HIGHWAY DEPARTMENT—*page 43, below; page 68.*

ROBERT SHANGLE—*page 9; page 10; page 11, above; page 11, below; page 14, above; page 14, below; page 18, above; page 19; page 22, above; page 23; page 23; page 30, below; page 36; page 37, above;; page 40, above; page 41; page 42; page 43, above; page 46, above; page 46, below; page 47; page 50, above; page 52, above; page 52, below; page 53; page 54, above; page 55; page 56; page 57, above; page 61; page 69, above.*

STAN THOMPSON—*pages 44-45; page 27; page 57, below.*

SAM AND BRUCE WHITE—*page 25, above; pages 48-49; page 72.*

(Following page) Portland's heritage as a river city is evident in this peaceful riverbank scene on Sauvies Island.

SEA QUEEN
CML
CROWLEY
SEA QUEEN
SAN FRANCISCO